Am I a Good Father?

AL PIZARRO

authorHOUSE

AuthorHouse™
1663 Liberty Drive
Bloomington, IN 47403
www.authorhouse.com
Phone: 833-262-8899

Published by AuthorHouse 03/08/2021

ISBN: 978-1-7283-0736-7 (sc)
ISBN: 978-1-7283-0735-0 (e)

CONTENTS

WHO AM I

It's so funny or maybe not so much since I'm still going through stuff as I start to write this book. I've been thinking about this for the last year. All the things that could've prevented me to write this book has happened to me. So yes I'm writing this book during one of my storms, issues, problems whatever you want to title it. We go through so many things in life that we have learnt, to just label things. It makes it kind of easier to deal with, so we make excuses in order not to finish what we started. To begin with, let me make this clear, you can't achieve anything that you want without this one important item and as I get to mention it I'm already feeling you saying well here we go another guy saying GOD/ALLAH/JEHOVA/ABA yeah but that is the answer. So let's begin, this is my story, my inner most thoughts, my interpretations of what helped me. So close the book, walk away and move on if you already have that thought in your head. Here goes another Christian, Muslim, Jew, Buddhist saying GOD will help you, because that is the answer!

As a man growing up in the South Bronx which doesn't matter, but some people believe that it does, wherever you come from. Rich, poor, middle class, Asian, Muslim, Christian, Catholic, Jewish I don't care, it applies to you. I will go even further Gay, Bi, Transvestites, Transgender whoever. All you need to understand, is that if you want to do better for your children, biological or adopted, step children or

your neighbor's kids. The desire that's always pushing you, to try to be better, or can you be better, you even question yourself, if you can even be a Father, we not even talking about being good, just handling being a parent. Our mind, heart and emotions are constantly battling whether we can make it. I Am A Good Father is always the question we ask ourself, can I do better, I've done the best I can, I need to do more or how about, I can't do it by myself still another phrase. "What do you expect I'm a Man". We think that we have all the time in the world to teach, show, correct, share everything to our children. In reality we really pass the responsibility to others as soon as we get the chance. Isn't that true? I mean we have to work, sleep, have time for ourselves, our spouse, if you have one, your family, friends our habits, old and new. So how much time do you spend with your children after all that.

My pastor once told me that I gave him the most precious thing a person can ever give someone. I wonder what can that be, there he was laying in a hospital bed after another heart attack and I'm still selfish. Telling GOD I need this man, he has shown me so much in a short time, don't take him away. So I was still thinking about myself, wow didn't I learn anything. I didn't know it then but now I have more peace that brings me more clarity and a better understanding of myself. Let's get to my pastor, so my pastor tells me I gave him my time everyday going to see him at the hospital, reading the bible to him, praying with him. Time a concept that I'm aware of but never looked at it from his point of view. I was a kid from the hood, the projects, drugs, alcohol, selfish, arrogant, proud, angry, tough, a member of a several gangs from age 13 - 26 and I would've done whatever I had to in order to make it. A good time to me was going out on a Friday and Saturday and having the money to have drinks, get high and get laid. I didn't care if I hurt people in the process and forgetting two very important things, GOD and family. Yeah I use to hear that all the time but I never really applied it. I had an excuse for that too, you know I went to church on Easter Sunday, Ash Wednesday and Palm Sundays. So yeah I believe in GOD and Family, yeah I was that man I had to have several woman one(1) wasn't good enough. Living everyday having fun, why not, I was a grown man now, had a job, a business, what more can I ask for. Time, all I did was waste it, but a had a lot of fun or did I? I still misused it, abused it just through that time way. Like I had all the time in the world, now when I look back I could've spent more time with my children, building a stronger foundation, teaching them more. So the pastor was right, that time was gone and I couldn't get it back.

So it's the most valuable commodity we squander and we don't even know how much of it we have, kinda reckless right? These are some of the things we believe we're doing right in how we use our time while with our children. So your home with your kids you're baby sitting, because you're the every other weekend dad and your child is in the bedroom or living room or outside playing. In the meantime you are on your playstation, X Box, working in your garage, watching the TV. I mean you're watching your child right!. Or how about you're watching something on that you don't want to be disturb. Hey you're still home so what's wrong with that. Now it could be that you're just laying down in bed tired so you figure I'll sleep a little while you're still watching the kids right. No it's not right! You're not spending time with your children, you're selfish and are thinking about your own needs. The time you have with your children should be just that simple, be with them, talk to them, hold them, laugh with them, play with them, teach them, love them. Now I'm not saying you don't love them, I'm just saying, how do you use your time when you are around them?

Getting high drinking or doing drugs is another waste of time. Yeah I had a great time, I spent most of the time trying to feel a certain way, that buzz you want or I just need a couple of hits to help me feel better. So now we need to self medicate ourselves to feel better. Is there something wrong with us that we have to feel better or we just don't like who we are when we are sober minded. Being high on whatever is like living on the outside of reality without really facing it sober minded and I you had all the justification, all the excuses. It's just a couple of drinks, what's a little weed, a couple of hits of blow. Who can it hurt, everyone is doing it and so what I sleep a little less. I can go to work on two hours sleep, I need to enjoy life I'm not going to work all my life and not have fun. Sounds similar. We are Fathers, role models, leaders, protectors, caretakers. Tell me how would you like to send your kids to the baby sitter knowing that they're getting high, drinking, playing video games or sleeping while you pay them to baby sit.

Well, if any of this relates to you, then keep reading because I don't just stop there. I want to go deeper or don't close the book. Just walk away from this. It's just the first chapter, no biggie don't need someone reminding you something you don't even admit, telling you how I use your time. Well guess what, I'm not telling you how to you your time I'm just telling how I used mine. So even though we feel we deserve to get high, got out to have a couple of drinks with the fellas, watch TV all day, or play video games. It's important that we look at ourselves. Ask ourselves have I isolated myself from my children for my instant gratification. Drugs/alcohol are not the only habits we replace when using our time during our life and we don't even realize it. Except when our other half tells us stop playing the video games and check on the kids or can you turn off the tv and go play with your children. That's a big hint something is wrong with how you handle your time. If its said enough times, you know this is not building you up but breaking you down. Your time with your kids are precious you never get it that back. I want to mention a couple of more items that needs to be said. Think about this, when you were sick and in bed do you over play it, did you really need to stay in bed all day or did you use that as a means to just have our own day without anyone bothering you. Here's another one on the computer where we stay there for hours. Once again something to stay away from our children keeping to ourselves. How many times have you said leave me alone, Im on the computer. As technology increases we get more distant and our tendencies are to get the new gadgets so more time to spend on them. Now there are some of us that feel we don't need the gadgets we can do it old school so you go out take a walk some a cig, cigar, blunt or take a drive. The point is you are not using the time you have with your children when you have time available. So old school or new school it still applies to you. The process of learning, using these devices take up more of our time. So they're less time to spend with our children. So let's go back to my pastor. He explained to me I have given him this gift because it cannot be reversed, taken back, it's gone, done. Wow that blows me away as I say it, so my pastor, my spiritual mentor told me I gave him a great gift. He died later that year I miss him still to this day, but here I am writing about what I've learned from many people that GOD used to change me. So I can be a better father and I'm still learning. So how much time do you give your kids young and old? Time is one of the greatest gifts we can give our children. I hope this book gives you insight, clarity, strength, a sober mind to live in this world as the best father you can be and yes I believe you will always ask yourself, am I a good father?

WHAT I NEEDED

S o this is not a how-to book, it's just an accounting of what worked for me and yes I know what worked for me, doesn't mean it'll work for you. Is there a kink in your way of thinking? Remember I said you need GOD, so yes GOD works for everyone. You can dismiss it and ignore it, or you can continue like you've been doing. As for me I needed a change for the better. After facing the challenges as a Father both with a spouse 10 years and as single parent for 13 years. I have been on both sides of the fence and I can say I've learned more from being a single parent. There was no two thoughts or ideas coming from the same source (Parents). I needed to learn from other men, fathers that shared my struggles or more. Fathers that came from my walk and those that had nothing in common with me. I was able to see that opportunity when I became a single parent. Before that the only Fathers I knew growing up was mine and uncles and friends of my parents. They were far from normal either drinking working too many hours or stuck watching TV. So my first introduction to what seems to be a healthy normal family was those portrayed on TV as I was growing up. I wanted that life, that family, that neighborhood but that was not my reality. I watch Father Knows Best, Brady Bunch, Eight is Enough and Good Times then I noticed. The white TV family had more of a family structure where good times kinda reminded me of a part of my life. Who the hell wants to watch TV and see the hardship and struggle I go through everyday not me. Even though some shows were just some fantasies that

I could not accomplish or were too far for me to reach at that time. I still had hope and dreams, others were not even on my radar but that's what I saw the happy family, big house two cars, family vacation. All the things I didn't have and wanted and then there was Good Times a bleak look into a different world as it portrays the family living in the projects hardship, struggles and pitfalls. My point is this was 30 years ago and the producers had no clue what struggles we go through. Now we have reality shows Jerry Springer and Maury Povich and these shows highlight the worst of us as Fathers, men, head of household. The sad thing is the rating for those shows are high and we are part of the reason it is. As we watch Father's and Mothers displayed on national TV all the different ways of how we screw up. We laugh and watch them but are we laughing at them or our own lives. So yeah there is a problem, there are not enough men helping men and the system adds to this dilemma.

The family court system that has a one sided version of fathers, where we are considered deadbeat dads before we even see a judge. It just seems like the odds are against us every which way we turn. Now I can say that yes, there are ways to avoid these pitfalls or get out of them and yes the odds are not against us. However the ways to get out of it or prevent them are more difficult. It's just a harder road we face, you need to remember we are paving the path for others to follow or learn. Our destiny were set for us before we were born. Yes we heard them as we grew up, he will the first doctor, lawyer, cop, electrician, etc. Whatever our family parents, grandparents, foster parent whoever it may be in our life perceived in their minds. So we already had a task we didn't sign up for and the stakes are high since we have been told we are the man of the house take care of your mom, brother, sister the list goes on. Of course how can I forget your are the oldest, youngest, smartest, brighter the anointing is with you, GOD has blessed you. Yep the expectation are high and you think that we don't need tools to get there, mentors to help us, a support system to back us up, think again. Here's a simple thought when we leave the education system whether you finish College, High school, public school or in the military. Where are all the tools we need to be a better father. I read all the books, saw all the TV shows, got on the computer. My dad if I had one showed me what he knew, my friend's dad showed more and of course family members. It just wasn't enough until I meet men that had one goal in mind. To teach other men to become a better man, father and they weren't perfect of course. Each man had something to offer me, show me, teach me and guess what they wanted nothing in return. So I couldn't figure it out why would they help me what's in it for them. They had the foresight to invest me so I can invest in others. What if I didn't care about others, they don't know me from atoms. What guarantee did they have that I would follow through. Share what I've learned become like them I don't know if I have but. I can clearly say to you, yes you need someone, yes you need a circle of men around you. Men that are better, smarter, more understanding, knowledgable, stronger. Yes I said it, I know you think you're the man and you don't need other men in fact you're doing great on you own. Believe me that's what I thought, but after meeting these men I felt differently. We learn from each other but more important we help each other, cry to each other, strengthen each other, consul each other protect each other. So even though these are in your life and do remarkable things for you. Yes you will hurt them, lie to them, cheat them, hate them, be jealousy of them, envy them and love them and when they die you will miss them. They will help you grow, learn not to lie, not to cheat, not to hurt your family or other's and you will learn to love them. Because you can learn to love your children better through their mentorship. So even though your children will lie, they will hurt you, they will hate you at times, they won't talk to you and they'll seldom see you. Ohh so you're the one saying I don't have those problems with my kids. Yeah so they smoke a little weed, have some drinks, he hit his woman now and then or she hits her man, they go out for days and come back with no explanations. Can I go on, yes of course i can, he has more than 1 baby mama, locked up, always working never has time to visit, moved from the neighborhood, state, country in the military. We are talking about grown men even though they are you son or daughters. So my job as a Father is done from childhood to adulthood. That is one of the biggest mistakes we make. We are their fathers, they need us all through their life regardless what that they think. So yes, we need to surround ourselves with righteous men, that have those qualities that we don't have but we need or want. It just doesn't stop there we need to have someone to applied those thing we've learned, and someone to teach. That's how we become better father's our education never finishes on fatherhood. Our walk as men starts spiritually and ends up right smack in the middle of our current life situation. So I don't care if your in jail, still getting high or angry. You need men to help you, work with you, sharpen you and if you look around most strong men are GODLY men. Look at Martin Luther King, Malcolm X, John F Kennedy, Hermes Carraballo there's a big list, check it for yourself.

WE DON'T NEED ANYONE?

One of the hardest things I had to face was my own stubbornness and pride. We are so blinded by ourselves that you can't see what in front of you. Pride will stop you from asking for money to feed your family or not letting your neighbor know your lights are off because you can't pay your Con Ed. Pride will stop you to ask for forgiveness. So you refuse to asked for help yet throughout your whole life you were taught to call mom & dad if you needed anything. When did we decide that we know enough or don't need anyone now. You don't raise your hands to ask a question even if you don't understand something. Are we too stubborn or too prideful that all of a sudden the switch is turned off and we believe we are now in a place that we don't have to do that anymore. Are we all grown up, that as adults we say to ourselves we have our own family, we're parents now, so we don't need to ask for help?. So what I screwed up and now I'm trying to make up for past mistakes because of my pride. Fatherhood has many different paths. You could be that every other weekend dad which by the way sucks big time. Or the dad that's just works a lot to provide for his family. Even a dad that's away, a military, or job related out of state dad. Or the dad that blames the mom for all the mistakes and still is the mom and dad in order to raise our kids. Sometimes pride and stubbornness brings you to that place. Where we are facing new issues raising our kids by ourselves where you have to realize that the mom is still very much in the picture. So because of our anger that fuels our stubborn ness we become less thoughtful. So yes under certain circumstances we need to ask for help from our ex-wife even though every part of our body says no. So there is specific person or person that we can turn to for help. Help is help it doesn't come with a handbook. It just very simple to do drop your stubborn and prideful ways and get the help you need. We should never have to turn that switch off, we are always learning and yes we need to asked when we need help or don't understand or just need to have someone with you. Fathers are set up as leaders, problem solvers, strong but how can you do that by yourself. Can you imagine TD Jakes doing everything by himself, or General Patton, or Obama you get what I'm saying. They all had advisors, counselors, staff, people around them that made them better at what they did. I know you're probably saying yeah well I don't have a staff or counselors etc. Sorry but you do, you just don't reach out to them, Close friends, co-workers, family. You know that gut feeling you get when you want to call somebody or knock on that neighbor's door. That's the time to be a real father, lets face it we don't know everything. One of the things that makes a good father is that time!, when you ask for the help, so you can be a better father. Whether it's learning to comb your daughter hair or help your son repair his bike. When you don't know ask and please don't just ship your kids to the neighbor house or say go to Julio house maybe he can help you. Who's Julio or Bob, or Ali everyone father has on in their life. That the person that can do things you can't or don't know how to. That's a band aide to the problem not a solution, It's time we realize that we are always learning and growing so if we don't raise our hands up for that added help. We'll, we just won't know how to fix that or know the answer to that. Sometimes we just say I'm busy right now I promise I'll do it later. Those small broken promises build up to a large foundation of don't go to dad because you know what he's going to say. Our pride is something that has been poured into us since childhood. Our parents or our grandparents instill this in us. That we are the strength and the leader of our family. This type of constant flow of what is expected from us doesn't help us when we do fail. We automatically think that we are failures because we were already told that we can't fail. Instead of yeah, you're going to fail but it's about you getting up and reviewing why you failed and keep trying until you figure it out. Always remembering that there will be times that it's just not meant to be. So if you stop because to tried everything, understand that regret can come back and hurt you later on in life. So make sure that you can live with your decision so you don't live with regret the rest of your life. We were made to work with one another especially with other men, to improve, to learn and to understand better. So we better serve and help our family, children, spouse. So pride is good if its balance and not used as a divider but a building block of your life. Sometime we are boastful about certain things where it looks like where proud but it becomes that ugly side of pride. Bragging about your achievements making someone else feel smaller even your own children. Be humble keep your pride in check, Its better when someone talks about you than you talking about yourself. No wonder why pride is considered sin it is easily twisted to justify our actions. Most sins are just that something that can modified to argue your case, that you are right. Yes, you can say I'm proud to be black or I'm proud to be a mother but when that is hurting someone else it's not working for their better good. It's creating a division between yourself and others because you make them feel less than. When you should be grateful that you are Black/Puerto Rican, Dominican or a mother. The fact you feel that you can actually do it by yourself is the problem. When you have no choice then you're in the right place however when given choice and you isolate everyone else PRIDE wins. Ask yourself why is it when you accomplish something huge you look for someone to tell it to PRIDE. Be humble each one teach one, help one, learn from one just be a better father isn't that a difficult task enough.

GENERATION X

It's funny that this generation of children are more informed and have access to the world via the internet. Is this a blessing for us as fathers or is it curse. I see it as more as a distraction, as we give more to our children at an early age. They embrace this knowledge and want to learn more from it. With disregard as to the time they spend away from us (fathers) family or friends. Also that fact that a lot of the knowledge they learner their minds cannot grasp them completely. We grew in an era that we were constantly in need of family and friends. Yet we see less of them or just isolate ourselves because we can't deal with the emotional wave that hits us. Some time ago when we were younger, our parents told us to go outside to play. We went outside and knew that at 12noon, 5-6pm we needed to be home for lunch or dinner. Today isolation is more common since you can play with your games, computer or phone and not talk to a single soul in the house all day. We have dinner in bedrooms not at the dinner table. So we thought it was hard enough to communicate with our children then, now it's worst. If you don't play any of the games or have a lack of knowledge in technology it's worst. I always remember visiting my cousins and hanging out with them when all the adults told us to go out and play or go to the room with your cousins. Those were great times you looked forward to the visits especially if you got along with those family members. This generation X is different, changing or convincing yourself that it's okay to be alone for a while or not see family for some

13

time. There is a lack of tradition, or obligation, the sense of duty or doing the right thing. It's more about what they want can do for themselves with no regards to anyone else. We live in a world of instant gratification the I want it now without working hard for it. They come down get some food and go back to their rooms if the space allows it, or go to the living room play a game or use their phones, tablets, computers. generation X is something we are dealing with now, learning how to know more about our children with all the barriers, like the digital divide. It's like they think the X is something extra they have and we don't. I believe that the X is actually something that is left out. generation X because there are missing something because they don't have it. Loyalty, compassion, respect of yourself and of time, when you're late or don't show up that person losses respect for you. They can no longer depend on you, why is it they are always late or don't show up. So you loss respect for that person and on the flip side the person may not even notice because remember it's generation X. So I was late I didn't show up I had something more important to do again, no problem in Justifying it. The problem will never be about them because they have a legitimate excuse most of the time so they believe. So are we not enabling the generation X as we move forward to advance ourselves. This generation has all the bells and whistles, they can see the world from their phones so why go out to experience it. Their ability to socialize are contain to facebook, instagram, twitter and texting etc. Let me know if your child allows you enter their facebook, instagram, twitter page. If they do don't think twice they don't have another account with an aka. This is the generation of secrets of skeletons in the closets before they every understand the traps they set out for themselves. The post pictures, say things and view things on the internet that we as Fathers would be ashamed of those things. Generation X has replaced learning from parents to learning from the internet, the world. They now say, dad you don't know anything, because they have the world in their hands. So we need to become the Fathers that adapts and learns from the digital world and the information that lays there. To all fathers the world is changing rapidly so don't stay stuck in your timeline. It's great to hold on to tradition that keeps the core value of what you know is good. At the same time learning new things like we were back in school.

SEPARATION

We grow up thinking about raising our kids and some parents may even think about how soon can I get them out of the house. Any separation will be hurtful in most cases, death, loss, or just a bad decision to separate will hurt. Some hurts are short term and some are long terms, some last a lifetime if you're not aware. Let's talk about those that are life terms. Yes those separations that will live with you for the rest of your lives. If your dad or mom dies, no-one is really ready for that it a hurt that we did not choose. Now as a father when that happens wow! it's like a wake up call. How do I go on without this teacher, mentor, friend, if your parents had that kind of relationship with you. You may have had a father or dad that was the worse no relationship at all. Because of a fallout, argument, disagreement, job or you moved to a different location and stay out of touch. You still can't bring closure to those things you wanted to address, now it's too late. You live on with the thoughts of should've, could've, would've done these things differently. Or what if you're looking back and see that you are acting just like the dad, stubborn, not understanding. You never wanted to be like him, but you look back and reflect and see that you are. The fallout yes just like an atomic bomb that leaves radiation that spreads like wildfire. It's a domino effect on your siblings, sons, daughters, grandkids so on and so forth. Everyone is effected, some will blame you, others will hideaway and some you will never hear from again because your parents were the reason they were interacting with you in the first place. That's a hurt that will take time and a lot of praying to get through it, you kinda never forget. Now imagine your child leaving the nest before its time, they're out there in the world and you know that they are not ready yet. You tried to prepare them but no they just left, how do you help them or do they even want your help?. Let's add the outside interference the people that get involved with your children telling them yeah it's about time you left. Or comparing themselves with their lives or I was out the house at 16 and look at me. The problem with that is they inserted themselves into your life without any accountability through your kids. They went on and suggested, guided and just bluntly said screw your dad I have better advice, I can guide you. Who are they kidding I'm the dad I will die for my child, will they? of course not. I could go on about this but I wanted to get straight to the point. A good dad will always look to do more. Now one of the worse kinds of separation I believe is when you tell your children to leave. Now this may have been a good decision but it still hurts just the same, some sendoff are, I'm not going to deal with you anymore. I can't handle all this drama, it could be that I want my own space and you're old enough to do your own thing. Is there actually an age when they have to leave the house 16, 17,18 I wonder. Or would it be better just to make that decision base on the circumstances. The truth is there is no exact age so don't drink the kool-Aid and allow society dictate your decision. Because that decision will haunt you if you did it for your own selfish reasons. My opinion is keep the communication even if you disagree with their actions, words or lifestyle. When they call or knock on the door, send you an email or text you, answer them. That might be the day they need to hear your voice, your wisdom or your apology. Separation is not healthy for any family, you are stronger together, agree to disagree, do not compromise on values that are the fabric of your life. Now in today's age its very important to not judge them, that will only lead to a bigger divide. Listen to them and really listen so you can better understand and solve whatever problem it may be. Sometimes we have the tendencies to interrupt their words while they are saying them. So don't fall into the biggest trap of them all "You Never Listen". Digest everything they said and always remember that you don't have to answer questions right there and then if you'r not ready for it.

A FATHER'S DISCIPLINE

I f you're going to be a father, planing to be a father or want to be a father, you will need discipline whether you do a lot or very little its up to you. Of course you may be thinking yes I have to discipline my kids and make sure they do the right thing. We are not talking about your kids we are talking about you, your behavior, speech and mannerism. Just remember everyone's interpretation of the right thing is different. So let's just start with the norm. If you're not a father yet, the time has note arrived. So right now you hang with your friends, get high, get laid, go out and party, work, well you get the idea. Your day may start off with a blunt(joint) or drink whatever it may be or just a morning jog, the gym. You may work nights and start the day off late, you wake up late in the afternoon. Now you start your day a little later than most people. My point is everyone's day is different, from church going, to gym, sports or sleep in or just like to play games. When you become a father you either start the discipline part or you add it into the newly formed family, the choice may be is yours. Because depending on your circumstances your wife, or girlfriend my suggest things you need to do during the day. I'm just letting you know that things will change if you care enough about your child or children. These changes may not be ideal for you but a change for the sake of your children and yourself will happen. Some people don't like change, they want to still hang out with the guys. Go out to the nightclubs or bars. Go and play sports or part of group of men that have discussions and plan things out. There are many different lives a person may live before becoming a father and there is nothing wrong with that. You may see nothing wrong in what you're doing and who you hang out with or how much time you spend doing what ever it may be. When you become a father even sometime before the actual birth of your child things will start to change. Some of it will be your idea and some from others, regardless change is coming. Discipline has everything to do with what type of father you will become. Good discipline will make you a better father or the lack of it will make you a father that will have more difficulties ahead of you. Let's take this time to describe some of the types of fathers that you may become.

Fathers that lets the mother raise the kids and all you do is discipline.
Fathers that work come home watch tv then go to bed.
Fathers that commute to work and get back home in time to shower and hit the bed.
Fathers that work nights and sleep all day.
Fathers that work from home.
Fathers that don't work the mother works.
Fathers that exercise and eat right is a criteria in their life.
Fathers that family is crucial in his life.
Fathers that family is not a big deal.
Fathers that religion is important.
Fathers that religion is not a factor.
Fathers that eat sleeps and live politics
Fathers that hates the news.

So this give you a broad look at the different fathers and you most be wondering what does that have to do with fatherhood. Well, who you are and what you do and believe in will be some of the things you will want to teach your child. However your influence or the way you were or not raised may not be what the mother may feel is right or grandparents. That's right they have some input to, so this is when discipline plays a big role. You have to have the discipline to know when not interfere and when to step right into a situation. You have to know when too much religion is overboard or when to little is not enough. Now guess what!, if you don't discipline yourself someone will tell you either your own child or the close family circle or friends. Either way its just not a great feeling to be told not to do something you feel strongly about. Discipline what does that word really mean?, in the dictionary Discipline = the practice of training people to obey rules or code of behavior, using punishment to correct disobedience or a regimen that develops or improves a skill. Okay so lets go with improves a skill yes that's it we all want to be better father so we want to improve ourselves in this area. So will need to let go of some of things you use to do or tone it down especially if it's a bad habit. Getting high or drinking too much because this habit might be a like a cancer and eat its way to your kids. Of course you can't get high like you use to but who's to stop you. You Stop you!. You need to have that internal voice that keeps you focus on changing the things you use to do. Most people are the product of their environment, the people that they hang out with or the things they hear and see. So you need the discipline and curb that appetite you can't watch pornographic movies or videos all day or all night. Go out with your friends all the time and just go out for the weekend like you normally do. Many people will say you have a responsibility now but in today's world if you haven't notice everyone is in it for themselves. They pass the responsibility to services like day care, laundry, nanny's where they clean, fold you clothes and yes even people to clean your house. This has been going on for decades, GOD forbid that you have watch your children, wash the clothes and feed them. It's interfering with your football, baseball, soccer, tennis game or you just want to watch TV. It is the discipline within you that determines the growth of your children and the information they absorb from your words, actions and habits. You are the reality show! and they are watching you 24/7. Some children will take what you have and expand on it or hate that fact that you wake up so early while they friends are still sleeping. Discipline can be the smallest and make the biggest difference in someone life. It all depends on what it is, it begins with you, you're are no longer the teenager, young adult whatever you want to call yourself. People are depending on you, so imagine if people around you have something to say about your language, demeanor, house keeping and more, then you have to wonder why. Take a look of what they are saying and see if you can honestly be bias and confirm whether they are right or wrong. There are many schools that we and our children go to 1.

home school 2. academic school 3. outside schools 4. job schools 5. friends schools. Life in general is a big school and how you navigate through your life will result in good moments or struggles through many moments. So what you learn you take, then you start to apply it in your life without noticing it. Some people go through their whole life without care or even thought to ponder about these things. Is that you think?, about how much of me is getting pour into my children or even more important you don't pour enough into them. Discipline a key component for your life skills. If you notice I never mentioned in the chapter hitting you kids I do believe that they may deserve a spanking or two. Just don't be the father that uses that as the only solution. Spanking, or having a heavy hand could be used in a productive way not as an outlet to release your anger. It's a tool that should be used very seldom with a very compassionate mindset. This is not for everyone some people can't tell when to stop for myself I never hit my kids that was my choice no that they are adults they need to reevaluate. Whether I did the right thing or not at the time I did not want to lay hands on my children. I will go further into that in the next chapter. So as a father discipline is something you will need in order to be a more skillful, compassionate, understanding, loving father.

A FATHER'S ANGER

Some people will automatically say you're always angry or watch out for his anger and the best one is he can't control his anger. Anger is a confusing emotion that we carry some people keep in check and others well they lose it. Is it a necessary emotion as a father to exhibit, well it depends on who you talk to. Some people hit their kids, scream at them, punish them. Some people do nothing at all as if it doesn't matter. Are you the father that doesn't believe in hitting your kids or do you just punish them. If you go to a court of law it is the one item that they identify to lock a father up or keep a father from his children. Something which I don't agree with is the involvement of government in a parents life. I completely understand why the laws were made up. I just don't it if I have to discipline my child I should be able to. As long as it's not abusive and within the logic of the circumstances we as fathers should be able to do so. Now we even have anger management courses that are mandatory in some cases. The sad thing about is that there are thousands of cases of murders of wives, children, and boyfriends because of out of control anger. Many fathers have "Orders of Protection" against them because of their anger. So yes it's an emotion that has severe consequences to all parties involved. I'm not going to say that I have the answers, because I still have many questions, in regards to this. However I'm willing to talk about certain things you can think about. Our anger can come from our past, upbringing, our parents, siblings, friends or our culture. Even all that I mentioned I'm not

21

a therapist just another father trying to do the best I can. So if you can agree that if you do not put your anger in check, your anger will get you in some kind of trouble. I've learn that anger has many different faces the instant reaction, the planned out one and the one that just lingers until you blow up. Let's not forget that there is also the anger that you release when you think it appropriate. I like that one, even though sometimes you can be wrong on that one too. Words are spoken and you can't take it back it's done you've hurt somebody and at the time you meant everyone word. Now it's 10 minutes 20 minutes later even several days later and you have regrets. We also make big mistakes by making decisions while we are angry which can turn events into disasters. Most of the biggest mistakes we make can cost us our lives or freedom. There are people sitting in jail right now wishing they didn't do what they did, it was that moment of anger that lack of judgement. That put them in the situation they're in now. So let me not forget to mention that anger is a great source of fuel to make you complete or start on a positive task. That's right anger can be use in a positive direction so that's what I want to write about. How can I take my anger and create the fuel I need to move forward. First you have to know that you are in a state of anger and can you turn it into something good. Example let's take something simple your kids get caught stealing. Now you're angry because they did it and it's a reflection on you so can this be a teachable moment or do you yell at them, beat them, punish them or all three. Some people will just talk to them (Children) "why did you do that Johnny, you do know it's wrong to steal, go say you're sorry" how's that for a solution. Was that the solution to the problem and the problem is fixed. I think it's gonna take more than that but again its determined case by case. Some children you can tell something one time and they get, some you have to keep telling them over and over. If your like me, that doesn't like to repeat my words, this becomes a recurring problem. So let's get back to how can I turn my anger into something positive at the same time let them know I'm angry about what they did and let them learn from this experience. So let's review some of the options, why not use a couple of those items and also add that they will pay for the item through, house choirs or even better work it off if it was a store or business. They return the item and still have to pay for it in manual labor. The point is that you can be creative and not always take the short cut. Sometimes the longer time that it's on their mind, the possibility that they will do it again are slim none. No guarantees but it's another option there is always another option don't take the short cut, think about it before you act on it. The point is there is no right answer just pause and think before you do something drastic. Let's go to the extreme you wife leaves you and now there is another man raising your kids and you're very angry. Be the bigger man and understand that she is not yours to own and that you can still have a good relationship with your children and possibly even your ex who knows?. Just don't do what we read about in news when another father beats, kills maims their children/wife/boyfriend because they can't handle that fact they left them. This is a hot topic and rightly so, because of anger, many people are dead or lock up and many families, friends, neighbors and co-workers don't talk to each other or see each other because of anger. It is the major cause of so much destruction in the world today I myself did not talk to one of my ex business partner for 25 years because of the crap he did. Once I learned to work out my anger I was able to get past that and forgave him and myself. I felt great afterwards and started to work on ending all the anger I was holding on to. That felt great but there are always more issues to come so take the time and don't let your children become a product of your anger. Keep it in check do a report card on yourself and see where you're at with your anger, be honest with yourself. To all the mothers in the world one of most destructive reasons that fathers that don't stay in contact with their children are because mother keep the children away from them. This thought out way of getting back at the father has broken many families and has created a deep whole in many peoples lives. I've seen fathers that want to have a good relationship with kids but the mothers causes different barriers. Between visitation and holidays that later on will be destructive to all parties involved. This needs to stop not only are you destroying your family but opening the door for more of that type of behavior in the future from the children. If you can't resolve your relationship with the father don't purposely keep the children away from him. Or worse use the children in any way to hurt him. Keep him informed on medical, educational and family events or occurrences. This will help him as a father to come around and become a better father. If you push him away he may stay away and he may be a good father moving on with his new wife. However it may not be the same for his previous marriage because of past events.

POSSESSION

This may be stretch but I wanted to include this subject because it is relevant as a father sometime we take items from previous relationship, friendship, job, culture into our fatherhood and impose it on our children. For now let's just talk about inanimate objects a car, a bed, clothing or house. This item is personal to you, you've had it for many years and want to pass it down to your children, whether they want it or not you haven't even considered that. It's something that you care for or let say that it came from your father or mother and you want to pass it down. We live in a generation where tradition and items do not carry so much weight in today's age. So you want to give your gold chain, ring, car or even house to your children and guess what, they don't even want it. It bothers you because it's in your mind this was never going to be a problem. You probably spoke about it many times to your children, so when the times comes they are reluctant. It becomes more of a problem just in the giving it away than it was worth. It's hurtful to you and they may or may not feel that it's hurtful to them. For example you work all your life to buy this house and now you want to give it to your children. This has been your dream since you starting paying the mortgage and knowing that one day it will be theirs. Now your children all they want to do is sell it and if you have more than one child they want to spilt it between them. They're thinking about the money they can get from selling it. Or they just don't want to live in that area anymore so they have no use for it. Now on the other hand you and your wife see this as the place you raised them, a lot of history in this house it's part of them. How could they just sell it off, that's the bigger picture, a father can be very upset about this. This may be the first house for this family and you're thinking it can be passed on from generation to generation. Or even worse you had a fallen out with one of your children and as a tit for tat you exclude them from having possession of the house. Now you can see how a father decision can really open up some drama between father and children even after you past. I saw this happening to my own family it's hurtful, problematic and causes a ripple effect. You need to really talk to your children way before hand and discuss what you would like to do with said items. See if they are even on the same page as you are, they may not see the importance of it at all. Most children see the area has changed and don't even want to live in the area that they were raised when they moved out and they never look back. Some children want to travel or have a vision of living in a whole different country. In other words expect nothing and have that conversation, get clarity so no one get hurts in the process. All you want to do is give them something, a piece of you and you don't want it to hurt anyone. It's just a different world today the dynamics have changed where we used to play outside with each other we now play on iPhone, computer and tablets. Less personal, more people are less connected to items in this age. Look at world as a father you have to notice the changes as time goes by. When we use to live in age where you didn't throw anything away until it broke. In today's age all you need is the next generation of that item so even though the car works it's not a hybrid, not computerized, not the latest model. So they want it now! thats, instant gratification. That's the world of today, so even as I write this book the world is changing. So your prize possession that you have held on to for so many decades. May not be as valuable to your children or means as much to them as it does to you. So as a father we want to pass something down to our children talk to them at an early age. This also goes for those career jobs, just because you're a cop doesn't mean they are going to follow in your footsteps. Some fathers are already have everything planned for their children yes she's going to be a lawyer. Once they become adults they do have a mind of their own so they will speak their mind about the things they want. So possession can be a career besides an item especially if you have your own business. So many fathers dream about handing their business down to their children when they past away. Only to find out they have no interest in the family business. The pressure on fathers continues not only as the provider but also to past down the traditions or creations from one generation to another.

RELIGION

I really didn't want to get into this but since it made such a big difference to me I have to include it. So I'm not going to get into what religion or who's religion is better or truth because that would be another book entirely. All I want to talk about of how a Father's choice of religion can and will have an effect on your children. So let's just dive in and say that as head of the household regardless if your single parent or not. Your faith will be a foundation for yourself and your family. It's the one thing you will introduce your children to when they are young. Many families do not even see the issues from the beginning. Your child has no choice, you take your children along with you to the church, mosque or temple whatever religion it may be. The point is they follow your footsteps from babies to teenagers and some to adulthood. This is your faith your foundation I get it, I have my own belief so I stand with you. Now let's look at this from a different viewpoint now their older and they have questions about their faith. Now I know there are some faith you can question and some you don't dare or not allowed. Lets just say for that this a religion that you can't so just the fact they your children are questioning you about your religion. Already has you upset, like how dare they question GOD, ALLAH, JAHWAY, BUDA, Jehovah who ever it may be. I don't want to disrespect any religion I just want to a make a point. As a father you want the best for your children and your thoughts will create ideas that turn into actions. You didn't decide to make them go to church/temple/mosque because you wanted to hurt them.

27

No we wanted to help them, our intent is always to help but sometimes it does just the opposite. So the action is done, you have them going with you to church, temple, mosque their choice is not included of course there are explanations or excuses for your actions. This is the way it is my father was catholic my family is catholic so we are catholic. My family is jewish, this is our culture, this is the one true GOD/ALLAH/JAHWAY. Bottom line they have no option. So expect that when they do reach an age that they have their own thoughts on GOD/ALLAH/JAHWAY/BUDA/JEHOVAH. Regardless of how you may feel, now they have their own feeling and they will thrust that upon you. So because this is so touchy of an area your emotions and thoughts are going to be tested. Don't forget that what was good for you when you grew up may not be the same case now. Being a father is a tougher job today than many generations ago. Now being a good father is more challenging and depending of where you live at, culture and families values. All these thing can make a difference when you deal with your children and religion. Everyone in the neighborhood may be jewish so that what you've been around. Or you many live in a third world country where religion may be more of a survival choice because it comes with education and food. I'm not judging I'm expressing that fathers may make decision base on the different situation that they are in. So a religion can shape a father or confuse a child because some religion come with their numeric sets of rules. That you may or may not follow at home, that will or will not effect your children when they become adults. That fact that you think about this before you act is the conversation, fathers often act on things before thinking about it and some thoughts are just as simple as following the numeric table 1,2,3. My grandfather was Catholic, my father is Catholic so my children will be Catholic you see 1,2,3. However religion is not 1,2,3 as they describe the Holy Bible as the living word, so if that's the case how can religion be that simple. So being a logical father just kinda take a look from all sides before making a decision that will effect your children for the rest of their life or not. Remember that will converse with other children from other religions and faith so your views and information will not be the only ones they will hear. They will be question and challenged as to their faith and religion constantly so expect the unexpected and be prepared as a father should be to. To answer questions that you probably never would have with your parents when your children approach you.

APPEARANCE

W e as fathers need to keep a good appearance however lets just rewind a little bit. As young men some of us pride ourselves in getting the best clothes, haircuts, shoes sneakers, digital devices. Our mothers and fathers brought these for us and as we got older we worked and got our own. In some cases our fathers and mothers could not afford these items. The assumption is, if we look good have the newest phone TV, etc we're doing good. So we naturally think that person has less problems than us or no problems like we do. The perception is because we look good and have expensive things that we have things more together. Than the average family that could be far from the truth but as we say in the hood fake it to you make. That's concept has damaged many families because we follow that rule even if it hurts us or others. Now that I laid down the premise of this chapter lets dive right into why this is another important piece of am I a good father. We go out of our way to buy the newest Jordans, designer dress, cell phones, flat screen TV for our children and ourselves thinking that this is what life is about. When that's just window dressing, somewhere along the line we confused dressing or preparing our kids visually as the greatest achievement that we can do. That's far from the truth, think about it if you had basketball team. You have to buy them uniforms, sneakers so the better the uniform the better they can play sometimes that can help. So all basketball teams with excellent uniforms and sneakers would be killing it and winning all the games. It's the training and the teamwork along with the planning that makes the difference. As fathers and remember i'm not talking about all fathers just those that feel dressing up my kids and buying them expensive gifts is the solution and see themselves as great dad after the process. That's when forget we are their appearance we make people think we're a great dad when it is basic component that we exhibit to glorify our status. You can't say that you have never said any of these things. Yeah I just brought my kids the new Playstation, or I just get them the new iPhone and it cost me about $800, but you know anything for my kids. Now behind the scenes you may spend little or very little time with your kids. You may not even see them except of the holidays and depending if you're paying child support and going through the drama of trying to see your kids. You might just be mad because you work all week and after child support you barely have enough to survive. So you work another job and can't see your kids because you're constantly working. The thing is buying something is great however if you feel that your duty ends there your wrong. Making your children look the part doesn't mean that they are happy and loved. The more expensive the gift doesn't give you absolution in fact it creates two things 1) they'll always expect those types of gifts and 2) it sets a trap of disappointment when you can't them those gifts. So if you buy your kids great gifts but they sleep on the sofa or better yet you can't take out to the movies, play or museum. Read them a book play with them or just sit and talk from time to time. Then let people pat you on the back for the great job you're doing when you know the real deal. The created an appearance that you know is not really whats everyone sees. That's what many father do so they can hear their friends and other people compliment them on the good job they're doing as a dad. I once meet a father that his kids were all dress up, new iPhone, sneakers, clothes, I mean the kids had everything. I went to his house on a job and saw that his house was a disgrace dog feces, ruined furniture, and dirty clothes everywhere. Had I not went to house on a job related issue I would have never known. So the appearance that he gave me was wow that guy is really thinking of his kids great dad. After seeing what I saw I said how could they live this way it didn't make any sense. Then on the other hand it made all the sense in the world. You get applauded for the appearance you present on the outside and that build you so why stop if everyone is saying you're doing a great job. So let's be aware that if we want to project that image then we need to do it all, not just the cosmetics. Study time with them, play with them, encourage them, listen to them and protect them from yourself. Your ability to put out an appearance that's all good but there needs to be balance in all the areas would can handle. Knowing that your appearance can hurt your kids more and leave a residual stain in your own personality. If you're not doing the basic why pretend that you're a great dad. Don't show boat like you got it together and of course you don't. Show that you don't have it all together but working on it because its important to your kids. This will make more father realize that everything is reachable. That fathers can be great without the appearance. Its the love that really matters the time you spend that makes it worth while. Think about it review yourself do a report on yourself and be honest with yourself so you can make the right judgement calls. Whatever you seek to improve in your appearance will effect your children, also so keep pushing. Reach your goals and build that foundation of a realistic fact of who your are without all the smoke and mirrors.

REGRETS

As a father we think too much about regrets, should've, could've, would've. Which I feel is one of the most destructive memories we carry throughout our life. Our regrets can become luggage throughout our lives, we carry them unknowingly. So after much thought this is what I choose to do. Of course everyone makes their own choices, my choice helped me make it through the hard times with a better perspective and outcome. The funny thing about it, if you made choice with good intentions you should have no regrets and if you made those decisions with bad intentions you need to make peace with yourself or in short live with it. So regrets are something that can kill you or build you up, think about stress, worry and sorrow they lead to health issues beyond your control. So understand that regrets are something you are always going to have. How you choice to live with them is up to you. One of things that being a father brings, is the weight of people around you, your children, family, wife and friends. They expect a lot from you and can bring you down when you won't deliver or can't deliver. So it's a big load on you from the start, here's some of the things you've probably.

1. Now you're a father so you gotta change you know you have to take care of your family now
2. You're the man of the house
3. Having a child changes you

4. Now you have to grow up
5. Your family comes first
6. You make the decision

All these comments are true but imagine each man learning this and carry the weight of when something doesn't go right. Yeah it can be a bit overwhelming especially when your marriage is broken or you made choices that you are now the father of several children from different mothers. We are labeled, broken and ridiculed while having to continue our life regardless of the situation. So keeping in mind, that yeah we messed up, we still keep that regret in our memories that will haunt you and hurt your well being. If you don't turn it into fuel to move you forward. So your regrets will be a part of you, so don't use it to destroy yourself, learn from it, build yourself up from it. It's never too late to change or make up for those mistakes. Even though someone may have died, before you can apologize for your mistake, you can still bring some kind of closure through GOD, ALLAH, BUDA, JEHOVAH. That's why in the beginning of this book I mentioned GOD as a key component. When you think it can't be possible the LORD makes it possible. So don't keep those regrets that keep resurfacing whenever you get depress and going through a rough moment as a corrosive thought. Pray, meditate, consult and share but don't and I repeat don't continue to hurt yourself. If you recall that saying "if it doesn't kill you it will make you stronger". That's very evident, if you use those regrets as building blocks to build a stronger, wiser, smarter you. You are always going to have regrets welcome it as a new learning experience about to happen. Most people when they fall off a bike get back on and try again. Be that type of father that takes the time to understand what just happen and realize the different choices you could've made. So when the opportunity rises again you can make the right choice. We are bound to make mistake it what we learn from those mistakes that makes us a better father.

COMMUNICATION 12

So you might say to yourself I communicate with my children. As a father I have a good relationship with my kids at least that's what I thought. I love them, I talk to them, play with them and discipline them so what else is there. I take them out, buy them clothes, I provide for them. So I am a good communicator, really I do all of the above and more. So why are your children lying, acting out, keeping secrets and the list goes on. Don't you remember when you were a kid, didn't you feel your parents didn't have a clue of how you felt, what you were going through or even your needs. That still goes on today even more so, since technology has expanded in many different ways. Fathers have always been tagged as the last person most unlikely to understand what children are going through. Its that the mom really understands more or talks to them more. Let's really get a clear picture, in most households they stay home with the kids. For generations the man has gone out to work and the wife stood home watching the kids and all the other items that comes with house keeping. Which is a huge job on itself and this has built a division between fathers and their children which we enable it by telling our children to speak to your mother. Or telling our wives okay this is your department I work and pay the bills so you handle the kids. Especially when it's a girl we automatically push any questions or problems to the wife or closest women in your life. As men we tend to keep our mouth shut and as father we guard ourselves even more. Now it's more important to take the mantle and be both mom and dad in communicating with our children. Break the cycle of only mom can talk to our children and we do the discipline. Being a single parent for many years (13) I had to change the way I was raise to the circumstances before me. I had to be mom for them because that was my situation not that their mom was dead but she was not around. I don't know what you going through but learning to adapt to create a better environment for both yourself and your child or children will help you get through the difficult times. So open up that closed door of your mind and open it up to better help yourself and don't be afraid, your manhood is still intact. It's the method you use that changes, so you can better communicate with your kids. Taking them to the movies, park, beach, pool is not enough, actual conversation about them, listen to them, get to know them. Don't be one of those fathers that see your kids one way and then finds out that they are a different person outside of the house. For business I always said communication is the key. Now I know that in life communication is the key. So be a better listener and try to absorb as much of the conversation that you can. Sometimes it even good to wait a bit before responding too quick.

GOOD INFLUENCES

Fathers may sometimes may not have the greatest judgement, by placing our children in circumstances that will not be good for them. We forget that we turned from children, teenagers, young adults and adults without being a Father. In some situations you're a father and a teenager at that same time which creates that inner battle I want to do all the things my parents did not let me do or the things I dreamt of doing. How you able to that and be a Father, that's a thin tight rope. If you're not careful that are many pitfalls that you will create during the process of you following your needs or desires. Yes I get it, I want to go out, I want to party, I want to get high, I want to have fun, I want to travel, I want to make money. These are all your wants, but a child has needs, children need guidance, good experiences and to be taught right from wrong. If you are all about the "I WANTS" you are depriving your children from learning at a pace they can understand and apply. Instead you take them along with you as you fulfill your wants. I never wondered about taking make kids at a very your age to the movies to see a R rated movie because hey it's just a movie. I want to see that movie and no one is baby sitting my kids or I want to see that fight MMA or boxing. These are just some of the items I picked for this chapter but there are many. Like smoking weed, Pot, a Blunt around your kids, to you it's the norm but what are you doing to your kids. It's a direct exposure to drugs, getting high what ever your turn on is. I know that we now have all the reason to use marijuana medically so I applaud those lawmakers that made that happen. However where and when can make a difference in a child life. Yes evening drinking alcohol in front of them, so you're a drinker you don't get a free pass. Some families have generations of drinkers because they grew up in a house that exhibit that. As a Father you need to remember my wants are mine, not my child. As a Father we need to sacrifice those wants and desires for the betterment of our children well being. Pick a time and place, make it safe for all your love ones and most important don't model for them something that you know they are not ready for.

So focus on items that will build your child's soul, health, mind and moral compass. Good influences are the key to help you become a better father regardless of your age, there are things, places and people that can teach you and your children to become closer. Challenge yourself, can I restrain myself from getting high while in front or with my children. Can I take them to places that they would like rather than where I want to go. Can I let them learn something I have no clue about regardless that it shows them I don't know everything. That a time when you show your children that you are willing to learn something new. Can I just put them first and me afterwards and not to the point that I have regrets but that I have manage my time for myself and my wants. Without endangering the well being of my children health, mentally or physically state. Good influences can be people that you feel will let your children see a different way of life, housing, ability, work skills, different careers and people with ambition. I can go on with the many different things to talk about in this chapter. I just want to express whole heartily that your choice is important for what they eat, to what they see, hear and feel. Make those choices good influences so you all can grow together, think about when you about to embark on that trip, place or visit someone. Will this benefit my children or hurt them. If you know your friend is always drinking or getting high, do you want your children around that. Let me give you another example of something most families allow. So you tell your kids not to curse but you visit your friend house the normal language is Mother F… this and F.. that. That's different than you saying it's okay to curse when you get older. Who determines what age is older, when you child becomes a teenager he or she may feel they are old enough now to curse. This is not the question of age this is more the question of how you express yourself. Good influences help you build the character you want your child to have. I don't write about this because I'm think about it, but because I have been in those houses where my friends have acted in that manner. I decided to make a change to help my children become better human beings not that it will always worked. What I can say is that I did my part to help them decide what person they want to be. That's who a father should be a role model to help them make better choice because of who you are. So make the choice, think about the choice don't lose the opportunity to surround your children with good influences Church, school, community they all play a part. Our society is overwhelmed with people of different ways of expressing themselves. Acting and judging, talking without thinking just exhibiting ways that hurt people. So give your children a different perspective coming from the the good influences you created for them.

FATHER FIGURES

As we become fathers our fathers may not have been the best father in our lives and in some cases no fathers at all. For myself I had stepdads never meet my real father until my late 30's. So I'm very passionate about fatherhood and since I did not have a biological dad growing up. I had 2 step dads Carlos Mendez and Fernando Gomez both of them passed away. So to immediately clarify something they were both my dads as far as I'm concerned. One Carlos Mendez a body fender repair man that I knew throughout my childhood and Fernando Gomez worked as a union man in the Hotel business that I got to know during my adult life. Two different men entirely, so let talk about my dad Carlos Mendez I guess it must have been tough for him raising a child that wasn't his, in that time era early 60's that wasn't popular. We weren't too close but close enough that I admire him for what he was able to instill in me. Work hard and to provide and stay true to your word even if it hurts. At the same time he did things that I did not understand. It was only later in life that I got to appreciate those thing that stay with me to make me a better man. However growing up I did a lot of crap to myself and others. That as I got older I realize that I didn't like who I become. It's funny how you get to look back and think about things your parent did when you were younger. Things that you gave them a lot of grief and make it more difficult for them. In the summer he would take me to his garage every weekend to learn his craft which I have to admit he did very well. Everyone that wanted their car repaired came to

39

him and he had a client roster of illegal race car drivers that always went to him. Each car came out of his shop looking brand new his method was hard, but the quality was there. I hated being there I did not see the sense of working so hard getting so dirty and being so tired afterwards. I told him that to his face but he kept bringing me along. I even told him I will never work like him I will use my brains instead of what he's doing. I know that must've hurt him a lot. Now I silently thank him for that time that he out of his work day. Now Fernando Gomez my second dad was a hard working employee at a hotel chain worked everyday and was in a union and always showed his love even though, again I was not his child. His ability to be at every family birthday, Christmas, New Years etc… really was surprising since mom was really the one who organized such things. So between the both of them I was able to come away with part of them in my character. So father figures can be a very strong part in our foundation the actual building blocks of our own fatherhood. if we look in the right places, pastors, teachers, neighbors, fireman, policeman, celebrities and family members. Someone you look up to or someone that just in your life for a period. They play a big role in your ability to be a better father. The father we want to become, is like on the job training. That can be side tracked when you lose focus on what's important. So even though you want to be the Father that your kids admire, be a role model for them there are things that get in way. So for me in a brief period of my life, I never felt the need to have a role model but understood. I knew that I wanted to be more than a normal father to my kids I wanted to be a great father. Better than my stepdads and more than the dads I've meet. So I purposely looked at other dads how they treated their kids. Men that were in my life and how they acted and spoke to their kids. In order to obtain and build more qualities into myself. So I looked for that quality in other Fathers that I may not have but would like to acquire. Our life after school and during job is always a learning curve, think about it. If you never went boating and meet a friend who took you boating that's your first experience in acquiring that skill. So we never stop learning always gathering more knowledge and learning different skill sets. So having someone as a father figure is good but you have to keep in mind that no one is perfect so don't let the flaws keep you from seeing the strengths they have. I don't mean strong like muscles but certain aspects of their lifestyle can be something you want for yourself. Here are examples of what I mean.

1. The father that exercises
2. The father that Prays
3. The father that cleans
4. The father that laughs
5. The father that listens
6. The father that cries
7. The father that's compassionate
8. The father that keeps his word
9. The father that works
10. The father that's punctual
11. The father works consistently
12. The father that builds things
13. The father that fixes things
14. The father that plans
15. The father that hunts

So you get an idea the list is long just depends on what kind of father you want to be. I feel its easier when you see your friend, family or co-workers exhibiting these traits that you feel you can acquire. So father figures don't have to be a famous person just someone that has that trait you like. Let me just say that's it's okay to admire singers, rappers, movie stars as long as they have that positive influence for you. Father figures all around you if you look for them and pay attention.

LET THEM GROW UP

I must have heard this a million times "Hey let them grow up". From family members, friends, co-workings or just people that can't mind their business. Yeah wow does that sound like you, I know how to raise my kids and they need me, they don't know what they're doing. So this is a double edge sword because on one hand you're right and on the other they are. So let them grow up is to let them learn from their mistakes. To let them live their lives without interference without you always stepping in to fix their problems. What do you do, they're you kids, you can see the train wreck before it comes, shouldn't you warn them. Have you been told you're enabling them, how could they learn if your always there to fix their problems. Have you ever heard the phrase "Teachable Moment" Well that applies here but there's not a simple application or method that you can use to make it work. Sometime one child get the fundamentals of a solution and other it takes several times of showing them. The only person that can determine weather they need more hands on or not is you. Of course our children do not have all the life skill sets we've acquire throughout the years. However what if you're a young teenager yourself and you don't even have the skill sets yet. What are you going to do, first thing is don't be stubborn, keep an open mind.Tell yourself you don't know everything, put that pride in check. We already agreed that each child has their own level of learning. Their DNA is different then any other person since each person is unique. As to when they need less hands on or more, no one can tell you that because they are not their father or parent. Unless they are raising your child or children themselves their advice can be heard but not applied. Even as adults we still seek advice from our parents if there are still alive. We may not want to tell them we screwed up it's an uncomfortable situation but we do what we must. That's the hardest part, becoming the type of father where your child can come to you for advice anytime. As a Father we have many obstacles that can change the way you raise one child from another. Education, physical ability, habits, friends, ideology, disabilities, community, drugs, alcohol, females, males, competition. You see I just listed some of the things that might change the way you raise your child. Circumstances we'll make you change and also make you a better father or worst father. Yes one father or parent can be better than the other but that one Father that handles adversity easily when another father the may not have any adversity that the other father faced.

So let your children grow up according to their character, learning ability and tools that they have to work with. You can actually still be teaching your child when they are a grown adult in their 30's or 40's. I always heard educators or people in leadership roles, label people "adult Adolescents" meaning in kid in an adult body. There are many Father's caught with that label, when they run from their responsibility, always late, sleeping all the time, hangin out, partying. This is when a Father still needs to keep working on their issues. So even though they are over 21 they have not mastered those life skill sets needed as an adult. So when other say hey he's or she's a grown adult let them figure it out. Lets say there are more things you can show them, teach them, correct them. So there is no age limit when to stop being a Father or Mentor or teacher this is a life time job. Some require more maintenance than others some require more conversations than others but they will always require all the love. Let them grow up but always be available and in touch especially with today technology you can call, text, email, Skype, FaceTime, instagram or the old fashion way write a letter. Who knows what other technical advancements will occur to make it easier to reach out to your children. Fathers remember that as you do these things, your children will have children of their own and I hope they pick up some of the good things you taught them. Our job, our duty, our love is shown in a life long time frame not until they are 21.

THE SECOND COMING

As fathers we think that we are fathers 1x time only. The reality is that we maybe fathers several times because the amount of kids you fathered or had different relationships. As our kids get older and have their own children. We get that second opportunity to help our children with our grandchildren yeah! Now you're a grandfather and guess what, you should have more experience and knowledge to help your son or daughter. This is your second coming, your second chance to be a father again. With the title grandfather some may say, this means your kids had kids, but I say, it means you have risen to a higher understanding and knowledge of fatherhood. So you are bestowed the esteemed title of Grandfather. There are some children that will refuse to let their fathers get involved with their children because of past or current history. Or because of your lack of responsibility during the times you raised them. There are many different reason why this particular problem may exist. You were away in the military, locked up in jailed, traveling because of your job or you re-married. There are a loads to excuses or problems that can occur from any of these circumstances. I can understand know because I've gone through my own issues. So I speak from experience, I don't think it is healthy to give birth to a cancer like anger or hate that will justify not having your Father being part of their grandchildren lives. All the excuses in the world can't make for it, yeah he drinks, yeah he was abusive, yeah he was locked up, incarcerated. No matter what, he is still the grandfather of your kids and you're pushing your emotions about your dad to your kids. I didn't know my real father so how can I hate him if I didn't know him. Of course he wasn't in my life so I could be mad about that but i also don't know the circumstances that cause that. In some cases our father story has never been told correctly, some information was left out and as fathers we carry the weight of sharing the burden that we've been told, that span decades. He may have been a total asshole at one time, he may have made mistakes at one time. He may still make mistakes and continue to do so, that doesn't change that fact that he is still a grandfather. So as your fathers son, maybe one day you will give him the chance corrected himself. Don't let your anger get passed down, how will you forgive yourself for the walls you built. Between your father and your children that continues from generation to generation. You will never be able to fix what you create because you didn't know at that time the damage it would cause. Father's you may have the chance to show your children that you've change at your second coming. So don't think because you mess up your life and your children life, that you will not be able to make up for it. Second chances come in abundances, you just have to be alert and know when it arrives. When your chance comes around try to do your best to do better. Keep in mind baby steps don't try to be father of the year just be a better than you were. If you weren't there before be there now. If you always drank before don't drink now. If you were always angry be less angry now, take it for what it is. Another chance and don't think you know it all, being humble goes a long way. Be kind, gentle, loving, caring, understanding and most of all, be grateful. You're a father and your second coming has arrive take ownership of it, wear it like badge and walk proudly. Grandparents are sometimes more direct with their words and lead more assertively. So understand that your words carry a lot of weight because you grandkids have heard different stories from your children good and bad. Its up to you to make new stories with your grandchildren its up to you to show them a different person than the one they thought they were going to meet. So it doesn't matter what you did before, just what you are about to do now. They say insanity is when you keep doing the same over and over, expecting a different result. I say when you don't know anything else you keep doing the same thing because that's all you know. The phrase "you can't teach an old dog new trick is bullshit!. You can teach anyone as long as they want to learn. So as you embrace your second coming also learn some new skills everyday. Because you can and believe me, your grandkids will teach you as you teach them. Every little thing matter music, reading, playing, swimming, sports, exercise and telling stories when they are going to sleep. You have a trunkful of things that you can show them because you were and are a Father first and now you have a second coming. When all else fails I find that just being at the right place at the right time goes a long way.

DO THESE THINGS MATTERS

One of the most dramatic things that can happen to anyone is death. Yeah when our parents die or someone else that is real close to us dies. It can effect us in different ways, we can shut down, be angry, depress or runaway. As I grew up in the South Bronx death was a normal occurrence, so as a teenager I never gave death that much thought. Someone was always getting killed in the early 60's and in my block it was a regular tragedy. Stabbing, shooting, fights that was part of the neighborhood. So you can imagine a war ravaged country or drug infested country death is more in your face. Did I think I would live to see 50 or 60 no way. So here I am, now I can talk about this after much thought. Being a father changes your perspective on things and losing a father or mother will have lasting effect on you. As I mentioned before I had Stepdads so as I reflect on that time of my life I cannot help but think of their deaths and how it effected me and what you I do different. Was I ready when they passed away hell no and to tell the truth they weren't. In the hood most death do not occur naturally, the funerals are many because of the shooting, stabbings or accidents. In the latin community the family is closed knit so there a lot family members and a lot of crying. Arguments and regrets fill the room up with many different conversations what stood out to me, was the fact that most funerals family had set up a collection in order to cover the expenses. When I was younger this was a normal thing for me to see. Now that I'm older, that's the last burden I want my family to go through. Why is it that as minorities don't have it together when it comes to that portion of their lives. I know that not all minorities go through that it that way but enough that required me to mention it. So I imagined what would happen to my kids if I died. It struck me there is something wrong with this situation men, fathers are not preparing themselves for this. So back to the title of this chapter "Do These Things Matter" yes and yes again. You as a Father need to make sure you're insured so that your children are okay financially. So that your family can pick up the pieces a lot easier so they can recover and your death expenses will not be an extra burden on them. A life insurance policy is not for death, its for the life. It helps gives that extra security your family needs just because your young doesn't mean you don't need. Don't inflict more problems on your kids they just lost their dad. The following years for them is going to be difficult enough so make sure you have everything done. Plot, funeral expense and last will and testament yeah this is the time when everyone will lash out and say crappy things. This is the time you are not there to correct, stop, or intercede during the funeral, burial. So as a father make it your priority that everything you want done is financially secured and that your children don't have to carry a heavy weight. Now many people reading this book might say this is obvious, everyone knows to do that. if you have not seen what many of us have seen, in the hood, or experience this, then you really don't understand. I live this practically all my life, grown men, father's not prepared for this day "stop the cycle". A job life insurance is not enough because if you lose your job there goes your life insurance. So make sure you have investing in a policy that you are responsible for the payment regardless what job you have. Read all the documents and select a beneficiary that will adhere to your last request. As fathers we need to step up and set an example for others to follow. Poverty, low income, poor education that's no excuse. These things matter and if you don't set these thing up shame on you.

LIVE LIFE

I t's got to be the most common thing among men. We don't get regular health check ups and we don't check our prostate. Why is that? with women as soon as they get their period off to the GYN they go they start of life of navigating through the medical system. It become second nature to them to see their doctors, set up appointments and manage the household in the same manner. Now for men of course when we were younger our parents took us to the dentist and doctor appointment most of us hated it. We probably said to ourselves when I get older I don't need to go to the doctor unless i'm sick. However how do we know if were sick a little pain may something serious but we pay it no attention. I know for me while growing up my mom took me to the doctor, not my dad. I went and I was scared I didn't want a needle and forget about the dentist that was the last place I wanted to go to. So how can we take care of our kids if we have these phobia's of doctors we just dismiss the process. As I got older I didn't go to the doctor unless if it was absolutely without no doubt necessary. It was only after I was diagnosed with asthma that I started to get yearly check ups and my dentist 2x a year. Because of that I was able to lead a healthier life even so it was Angie (my wife) who really open my eyes on staying on top of your health. Them it occur to me how can I be a Father to my kids if I'm very sick or dead. What if I could have just prevented it all just by getting a physical. Even more so how can I truly enjoy my life with my children, family and friends. If I physically was unable able to participate in the simpler things in life running, swimming, reading, bicycling, walking, exercising. All due to the fact that I did not get a check up to prevent whatever illness I may have. There no way I can blame anyone but myself, so I felt encourage to write this chapter on our responsibility to stay as healthy as we can. We owe it to our children and grandchildren we owe to our wife and family. We owe it to ourselves we (fathers) have for too long allow ourselves to get sick because we didn't do our due diligences. Just like getting a job and proving for your children we have to take getting our yearly physical that serious. We have to watch what we eat and make sure we keep ourselves fit. Fathers are dying are a younger age and by record numbers because of their lack of making right choices. We don't give ourselves the chance to live longer because for some reason we feel immune to illnesses like we can live forever. That is not true and if you're first thought is I don't need to see a doctor I'm good. Even though you know you're not or you feel it's just whatever it may be a cough, slight pain or discomfort something you'll get over with in a couple of days. This is the exact attitude and thinking that many of us have died from or are sick right now because of it. Most illnesses can be prevented if it's caught in time. Being a father is making sure you're around to be one. Both of my stepdads would be alive today if they followed this bit of advice. So even though I can't bring them back I can at least feel better that I have put it out there for others to read or listen to. This is something you need to add on to the list of Am I A Good Father?. Don't take for granted the time you have on this earth, work everyday to help yourself become a healthier father. Make sure you pass this along to all your children let them understand that as you take this serious, you want them to do so also.

KEEP THE KID IN YOU

Being a father kinda comes with certain images or descriptions. Responsible, reliable, strong, knowledgeable, protective, provider, head of the family. He's the person in the family that everyone should go to when there's a problem or something you want to know. You hardly hear about a father who's funny or fun when describing them even though there are fathers like that. As we grow up we are the product of our environment and the people around us. if you lived in a country that just getting some food was a struggle. Then your probably teaching your kids to know the seriousness of eating everything on the plate and not wasting food. Being more conscious of what you spend your money on. If you grew up in a business like structure where your father had to wake up open the business and provide for your family. You more than likely had to help you father during those times and made sacrifices, that as a kid, keep you from your friends. You probably are more serious and more organized because of that. Now if you were in a situation where everyone in the family was in the household cooking, cleaning, building, working then you got to see your father interact and play a bigger role in the family tree. I know I am missing a lot of different types of fathers as i try to describe some of them. I just want to give you a clear idea of where i'm going with this. Our fathers are comprise of everything they learnt and what was around them. So as a father, a lot of use forgot how to be kids or just never had that chance to just be a kid. Circumstances beyond their control could give birth to things they can never imagine. So if a parent died at a young age and your father was the oldest when it occurred. Then he naturally would assume the position of the older brother and become the father to the younger siblings. So having fun and hangin out was not an option. Especially if he's a single parent like a mom that had to go out and work. All the things that are expected in fathers may not be the way he saw his life become, he may be ready or not. So because of his past, his situation, different tragedies his life has changed and now he has to be a father and all that comes with it. So keeping in mind that yes I have to protect, stay strong, be responsible, be reliable and provide. Doing all that matters is important but never forget that you need to enjoy life. So you need to add have fun in that list you can't be a person that's all about business or work or religion, whatever it may be. You need to know that you children are kids first and you want to make sure they enjoy their childhood. Have fun take them out to movies, amusement parks, picnics, concerts, plays, historical locations all and more. Have fun during the this time enjoy these moments that you could not do because of the different tragedies or misfortunes that occur during your childhood. Have fun within reasons because you only have one life. Don't let your children get caught up in your past problems or issues or fears. This will not only improve your relationship with you children. You'll also be building wonderful memories that would last a lifetime. If you never went to museum take your children with you and all of you enjoy the experience. If you never been to a concert and want to go, go with them don't just pay for it, go with them, just because you a father doesn't mean you kind not enjoy what they enjoy. Open you mind and allow the kid in you to surface and create those moments you thought were lost forever. You are never too old even if you're labeled old school or old fashion to experience new things. Start to show your children why it's important the keep that kid in you alive. I've meet too many Fathers that rather just allow your kids to go here and there by paying for it but not attending because it's a kid thing or it's a girl thing. The bottom line it's your children and spending as much time as you can with them is important. No don't justify your lack of participation and don't go because you feel uncomfortable. This is how you keep growing as a parent don't be a couch potato parent or health fanatic to your kids just because you are. Have fun with them, you know that this time in their life is important and you want to look back when they are adults and remember those times as if it were yesterday. Now for you Father that don't know how to shut off yeah I know those that always want to have fun it's always a party. Having fun responsible is enjoyable, it's life changing and memorable. Fun overload is disastrous it can cause a load of complications like, let's skip work, school, chores, pay bills. Let's have fun when we can do all those things later or one of the best lines what one day it's not going to kill us. Will I call it the slow disintegration of the basic structure of fatherhood. You don't even see it coming because you're having too much fun during those times. It's addictive to always want to do going out to the beach all day, when you come back home chores still not done. Went out last night woke up late and didn't move the car, that causes you a ticket. Just went out with your friends to blow some steam from the ordeals you went through during the week. Oops I forget to take my kids to practice or no milk in the fridge. It just becomes a domino effect of different things that can happen but you don't care because you had fun. So as I say in one way make sure you keep the kid in you and have fun with your children also keep it in check so it doesn't become a problem. When do you know that you are not causing a problem while having fun. When no one gets hurt and nothing suffers from the aftermath of the fun moment. So you still go work and you're at you best at work, you still drive to wherever and you're not falling asleep at the wheel. You can still spend and it didn't interfere with you daily, weekly, monthly bills. When you can afford the time and the money to do it. They are exceptions to this method but it can only be judge by yourself.

SOCIETY AND FATHERS, LAW AND COURT

I've have always remembered a time in my life when fathers were the pillars of the community. When the title fathers was held in high esteem. When fathers were respected throughout the family tree. This is no longer the case, what our system has done. Is taken a few bad fathers to represent all fathers and even gave them a title deadbeat dads. Where other cultures and countries honor their fathers this country has been chipping away this decade long title. To the point that fathers today believe the crap that's being feed to them. We have low esteem and fight the images that has been damaging to our families. These titles, deadbeat dads, lowlife, bum, bastard they become the labels when a relationship goes wrong. The system for a long time has tried to solve martial problems with a broad stroke. With terrible results leaving families broken and fathers being ridiculed, abused and financially destroyed. I say this because I have personally gone through the system of child support and fighting for custody of my children. Yeah there are dads that don't deserve the title of being a father but to use that one or several or thousands of them to represent the whole is not only unfair but an insult to each father that's doing the right thing. Because this process has now become a business for the state and the court system. They have enforce child support in a manner that has damage many fathers past or present. Where recovery is difficult and tiring, trying to rebuilt oneself in order to start over. Yeah I believe that you should support your child no matter how many they are. However the remedy that we have now has to be revamp because it is causing more problems daily and flowing into several generations of families. Many women don't want to solve their problems with their husband they rather get the child support. Why deal with a man is you can get a monthly check from his and eliminate his presence. Now again this is my view point from what I experience, more woman are having more children from multiple men. So they can get more of a monthly child support payment and live a better life. Men once they are charged with child support payment would rather work off the books so they can at least pay their rent, electric and other bills. Some fathers move back in with their parents in order to get back on their feet. So this system is broken and it needs to be reviewed to adjust a healthier way to solve this situation. It's causing more division between their kids and their family. This country this society has belittle Fathers and stomped on them until they can't get up by themselves. The pride, strength, focus is gone because you go a court system that is geared towards women and they don't listen to the fathers. They shoot them down and then take as much money as they can through the process. Not considering what is left for the father to survive. I had to speak about this because there is no way I could finish this book without putting this in. The city, state government has been in our lives to the point that's its disruptive. We are human being with emotions, feeling and love. Our skills or careers that we developed throughout the years are base on that financial goals we set for ourselves. So we can provide for our family, yeah a lot people make mistakes, but damn. Its like, they not only punish us for it, they brand us and label us which has a longer lasting effect on our well being. We become less than a father when we are damaged goods and now even if we try to start again with another family. We have to work two jobs or longer hours just to make ends meet. Fathers we are damn if we do and we are damn if we don't. Why is it that other countries and cultures don't have the broken family syndrome like we do. Its even noticeable in the holiday "Father's Day" not a big deal but "Mother's Day" holy cow that's the parent. Please understand I am not against women I believe that women should have all the opportunities men do. I support women in their endeavors and all the positions they hold. I'm just saying that we have to look at what the damage to father since this book is about fathers. Fathers have been put down to second place when we use to be first in the family tree. So many broken families, so many single moms. It's just heart breaking as I went to court to see the line outside all the around the court system with everyone fighting for their child and child support. There has to be a better way I don't have the answer or the solution. What I do have is my opinion that this has done more damage than good and something has to change. You (Courts, City, Government) have crushed so many fathers and continue to do so and expect fathers to brush it off like it's nothing. We can't brush it off if it happen, if it effected our life, finances and our pride, it's a hurt that doesn't just go away. While still respecting the single mother and understand the struggles. Now before child support, families had to work out their difference not just quit and collect the child support. They had to compromise and find a solution to the issues they are going through. Now the government just said here's a check and keep it moving. Not all problems can be solve with a check. Of course there are exceptions abusive fathers, drug abuse, father that don't take responsibility. That's what the system is for, not because I can't make this work, I rather just give up.

JUST BE A DAD

I hope this book made you think more about being a father, I know that I don't have all the answers but I do have many questions. Ones that always stay on my mind, did I do a good job as father or could I have done it better. Maybe I should have done things differently the truth is if you're thinking about that then you're on the right path. There is no secret formula or method on being a good dad it the process of trying that's important. There are too many variables involved with location, circumstances, and emotions that come into play. So what works for one person may not work for another and because you sent you children to best schools, home school, boarding schools. Doesn't mean they will turn out to be the best of the best. Or because you didn't send them to the best school that they will turn our worst. It's the love you show them, it's the time you give them and the sacrifices you make. It's that point when you do things for yourself and not for them. That time when you say enough of this bullshit I'm out, I quit, I don't want to deal. That's when the problems start and thats when you become less of the father you intended to be. It's important to stay strong, because you just don't know if tomorrow everything changes because you hung on in there. Timing is crucial, sometimes just because people tell you now's the time for you to do the dad thing. May not be the case at all, because deep down inside you know it's not for whatever reason. Your gut feeling is telling you it will fail. Sometimes just stay still, not making a choice will be the best choice.

So don't let people convince you to make choices that you will regret later on. Just be a dad, think of what you would have liked your own father to do when you were growing up. Or recall a moment when you dad was in the same predicament and made the wrong choice, so you know in good conscious you will fail in that endeavor or that task. When that same task can be done in a day, week or month. Just be a dad don't try the over reach just try to reach the goal that are obtainable. Bring back those day when people looked at fathers with admiration and respect. Hold your head up high and say to yourself. I'm a father now and I will be the best father I can be. Not what everyone else determines what is the best father. The ghetto, the job, your education, your family does not define you. You make the choices, so don't justify the options you have with circumstances. Make as many right choices that you can. I believe that 50% of being a dad is being there the other 50% is divided between providing, talking, listening and following through. So if you are there all the time 50% of you being a dad is done. Don't compete with others compete with yourself. Understand that you will be a father for a lifetime so you will be learning and teaching for a lifetime, it never stops and it shouldn't stop. So there is no time when you get to say to yourself or someone tells you okay you job is done. Just be a dad keep it simple, if you don't make million dollars, or have a fancy house, a college education. That doesn't keep you from being a good dad. You need a good heart, and GOD, ALLAH, ABA, JEHOVAH. Get all the help and guidance you can get read, listen and watch always apply your self, and you won't regret it.

Please pick up any of these books, they will help you as they helped me.

So You Call Yourself A Man - TD Jakes

The Blueprint - Kirk Franklin

Dedicated to GOD, my wife Angie, our children Alex, Angelina, Gaby, Lucian, Matthew, Nina, Victoria, my mom and Pastor Hermes Caraballo, Pastor Jose Rodriguez

Printed in the United States
by Baker & Taylor Publisher Services